Below the towering trees
of the dense rainforest
canopy of Central America,
a population the size of
New York City bustles.

Eight million sisters working together in one of the most ancient and complex societies on our planet.

A society of builders and soldiers, caretakers and cleaners, farmers and pharmacists,

and foragers that carry
leaf cuttings along a busy
highway back to the . . .

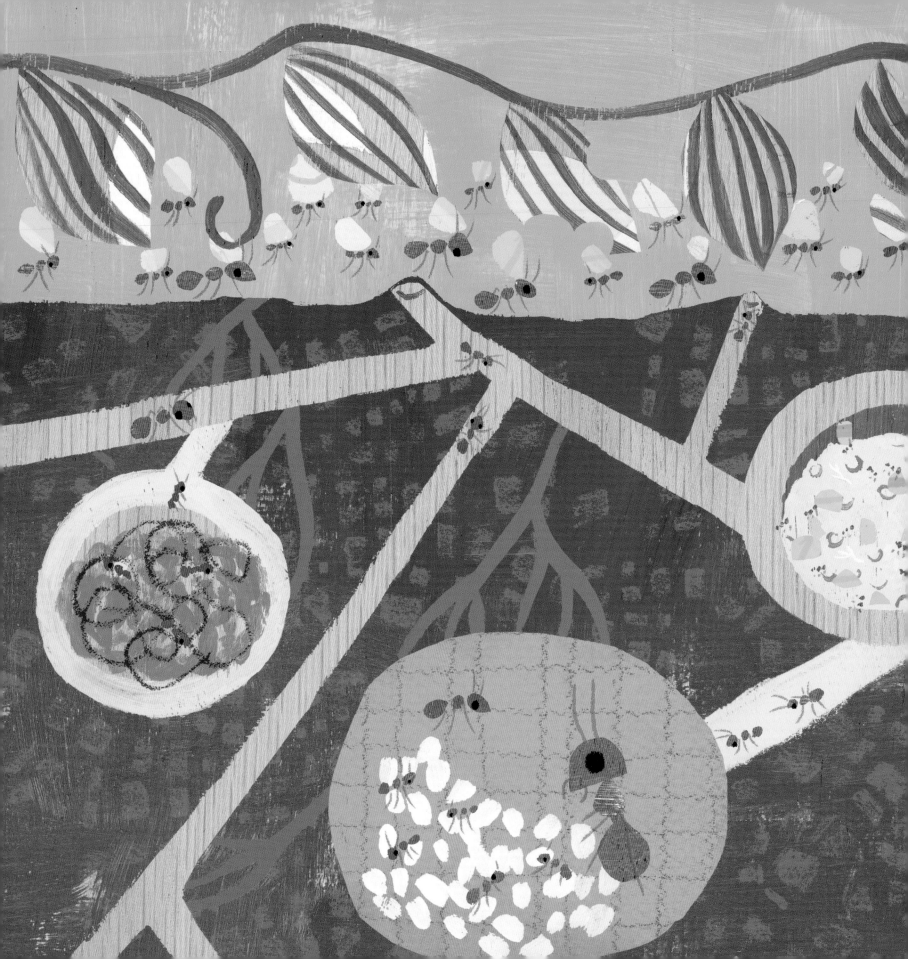

CITY OF LEAFCUTTER ANTS

A SUSTAINABLE SOCIETY OF MILLIONS

Amy Hevron

NEAL PORTER BOOKS

HOLIDAY HOUSE / NEW YORK

The city was founded one afternoon by a young leafcutter ant queen.

After a single mating flight, she burrowed into the soil and dug the city's first chamber.

In it, she laid a batch of eggs and placed fungus from her mother's nest, an essential ingredient for the new city's survival.

Over the years, the population boomed. And the queen's daughters developed different physical traits.

Soon, they organized into different jobs. Now, each plays a big role in helping the city thrive.

The youngest stay in the city
to work as caretakers.

They feed and tend to the
larvae and their mother in
the nursery chambers.

The oldest work in the garbage chambers, where they manage the city's trash, turning it over and over to help it decompose faster.

Down the road . . .

. . . tiny inspectors clean and
process leaf cuttings,

while small pharmacists use antibiotics
produced from their bodies to keep
the city free of disease.

Around the corner, midsized builders drill tunnels to circulate air and keep the city cool,

while others dig new highways
at careful angles to prevent
unwanted flooding.

Up ahead . . . something
else that's unwanted!

A poison dart frog!
Hungry for an all-you-can-eat
leafcutter ant buffet!

The work crews sound an alarm
by releasing a special pheromone.

Caution! Caution!

Large soldiers detect the warning signs with their antennae and rush in.

Equipped with powerful jaws that can cut through leather, they swarm the unwelcome visitor.

Forcing it up, up, and out . . .

Right into oncoming traffic!

Bystanders zig, zag to avoid collision.
Haulers skitter, scatter,
dropping their cargo.

The intruder limps away to
a neighboring bromeliad plant.

Above the hubbub, foraging crews
continue their work in the canopy.

They cut through leaves with chainsaw-like mandibles and sip on sweet leaf sap, but they do not eat the leaves.

Instead . . .

. . . they carry their leaf cuttings along a busy
highway, following their colony's trail . . .

. . . hauling enormous
weights at incredible
speeds back to the city.

Past builders and soldiers,

past caretakers and cleaners,

past inspectors and pharmacists.

And finally . . .

. . . to farmers that work in an isolated chamber where they chew the leaf cuttings into a paste and feed it to a fungus garden.

The garden that started from that first fungus now feeds the entire city of eight million.

Leafcutters belong to a group of ants that were our world's first farmers, growing industrial-scale food crops for over 60 million years.

And from the garden, an aspiring
young leafcutter ant queen takes
some fungal threads and tucks them
in a special pouch beneath her head.

Now her work begins.

She will leave the city, never to return.
Out on a single mating flight, and
then on to start a new city.

Out from where new plant
roots stretch to the rich soils
of chambers and highways.

Up to where new buds
bloom from pruned
branches and vines.

Toward the afternoon sun that
now floods through a new opening
in the dense rainforest canopy.

Above a bustling city of industrious
little workers . . .

. . . who play a big role in helping
the rainforest ecosystem thrive.

MORE ABOUT THE EXTRAORDINARY CITIES OF LEAFCUTTER ANTS

The sights and sounds of leafcutter ant cities can be found in the tropical rainforests of Central and South America. Their cities, known as nests, can house over 8 million residents and are architectural marvels with temperature-controlled chambers, industrial-scale indoor food crops, and pathways that prevent rain from flooding the city. One of these massive underground cities was unearthed in Brazil and found to span an area of 538 square feet, extending 26 feet deep and containing 2,000 chambers. In building such metropolises, these tiny workers play a big role in engineering the rainforest. They aerate the soil and redistribute nutrients underground, making the soil near their nest ten times more fertile, and their pruning of trees and shrubs stimulates plant growth and allows sunlight to reach lower parts of the dense rainforest.

Leafcutter ants are the rainforest's dominant herbivore and can defoliate a tree in twenty-four hours. These industrious foragers work in teams to collect leaves. Some workers cut, while some carry the leaf bits. Smaller workers ride on top to clean the leaves and ward off attacking flies. They collect leaves from plants that provide specific nutrients for their fungus garden. They are one of only a few animal species to cultivate their own food crop. And their ancestors were doing it since shortly after the dinosaurs went extinct.

Scientists are studying leafcutter ants' city structures, antibiotics, and waste management systems for possible use in human populations. But where tropical rainforests are being cleared to make way for farmland, leafcutter ants can be seen as pests. With their natural predators, like poison dart frogs and anteaters, being reduced in great numbers, the leafcutter ant populations are thriving. And where they can no longer forage from their native rainforests, they instead are adapting to forage from pastures and orchards.

Leafcutter ant cities are first established by a queen, who in her fifteen- to twenty-year lifespan continues to add to the city's population. The workers, all female, live three to seven months. Over the millennia, leafcutter ants have evolved to be highly polymorphic, meaning they have different physical traits. They are divided into four working castes: minims, minors, mediae, and majors. Each caste does a variety of jobs.

LEAFCUTTER ANT JOBS

Foragers—Foragers select specific plants, like oak, citrus, almond, and pepper plants. They cut and carry the leaf bits back to the nest in teams. They secrete chemicals from their poison sac glands to leave trails for their colony to follow.

Inspectors—Inspectors check and rid the leaf cuttings of parasites and unwanted pathogens.

Waste Management Workers—These oldest ants are divided into two groups. One crew collects the city's trash and drops it near the garbage chambers. The other crew stays in the chamber and tends to the garbage heap. These workers stay out of the rest of the city to prevent the spread of disease.

Farmers—These small ants can fit into the holes of the fungus garden to feed and care for it.

Pharmacists—Pharmacists use bacteria secreted from their bodies that function as antibiotics and antifungals to keep the leaves and garden free from disease.

Guards—These smaller ants ride on leaves to keep watch for parasitic flies.

Haulers—These large ants carry heavy loads and maintain pathways.

Soldiers—These ants have large jaws that lack poison but can cut through skin and leather. They defend against predators and other ant colonies.

Caretakers—Young ants care for larvae and their mother in the nursery chamber.

Queen—The queen mates during an annual "nuptial flight." Only two percent of queens survive the flight. The ones that do store 300 million sperm from this one-time event and continue to lay eggs over the rest of their lives. Once a city is established, a small number of larvae are given special diets so they will grow into potential queens.

Male Drones—When the annual mating flight nears, the queen will lay a small number of male larvae. These will grow into winged males whose sole job is to mate with new queens. The male drones die after the mating flight.

Selected bibliography

Buijs, Jasper. "Foraging and nesting habitats of leafcutter ants." Canadian Organization for Tropical Education and Rainforest Conservation, 2012. http://www.coterc.org/uploads/1/6/1/8/16182092/foraging_and_nesting_habits _of_the_leafcutter_ant.pdf

Carson, John Wade. "Foraging and nesting behavior of leafcutter ants (Atta cephalotes) in a tropical secondary forest" (2019). *Tropical Ecology and Conservation [Monteverde Institute]*. 454. https://digitalcommons.usf.edu/tropical_ecology/454

Foitzik, Susanne and Olaf Fritsche. *Empire of Ants: The Hidden Worlds and Extraordinary Lives of Earth's Tiny Conquerors*. The Experiment, 2021.

Landers, Jackson. "Were Ants the World's First Farmers?" *Smithsonian*, July 20, 2016. https://www.smithsonianmag.com/smithsonian-institution/were-ants-worlds -first-farmers-180959840

Swanson, Amanda C., et al. "Welcome to the *Atta* world: A framework for understanding the effects of leaf-cutter ants on ecosystem functions." British Ecological Society, March 6, 2019. https://besjournals.onlinelibrary.wiley.com/doi/10.1111/1365-2435.13319

Additional reading

Gerdeman, Beverly. *Ants for Kids: A Junior Scientist's Guide to Queens, Drones, and the Hidden World of Ants*. Rockridge Press, 2021.

Messner, Kate, and Chris Silas Neal. *Over and Under the Rainforest*. Chronicle Books, 2020.

Rzezak, Joanna. *1001 Ants*. Thames & Hudson, 2019.

Stewart, Melissa. *National Geographic Readers: Ants*. National Geographic Kids, 2010.

Active Wild, Leafcutter Ant Facts for Kids https://www.activewild.com/leafcutter-ant-facts-for-kids-and-adults/

San Diego Zoo, Wildlife Explorers https://kids.sandiegozoowildlifealliance.org/animals/leafcutter-ants

A NOTE FROM THE AUTHOR

I first became fascinated by leafcutter ants while on a trip to Costa Rica. During a hike through the rainforest, I saw highways of these little workers parading their leaf cuttings. I spent several minutes watching them and went back a second day just to watch them some more. Why were they carrying leaves? Where were they going? Why were they all different sizes? I had to find out more. With this book, I answer these questions and offer a peek into their extraordinary world.

To Lorie and John

A special thank you to Dr. Susanne Foitzik for her expertise on this project.

Neal Porter Books

Text and illustrations copyright © 2024 by Amy Hevron
All Rights Reserved
HOLIDAY HOUSE is registered in the U.S. Patent and Trademark Office.
Printed and bound in February 2024 at Leo Paper, Heshan, China.
The artwork for this book was created with acrylic paint on wood and paper, and digitally collaged.
Book design by Jennifer Browne
www.holidayhouse.com
First Edition
10 9 8 7 6 5 4 3 2 1

Library of Congress Cataloging-in-Publication Data is available.

ISBN: 978-0-8234-5318-4 (hardcover)